God Bless!

Make It Happen!

Make It Happen!

ERNST G. SCHMIDT

Introduction by Robert H. Schuller

Abingdon   Nashville

MAKE IT HAPPEN!

Copyright © 1976 by Abingdon

Library of Congress Cataloging in Publication Data

SCHMIDT, ERNST G 1931–
  Make it happen!
  1. Christian life—Lutheran authors. I. Title.
BV4501.2.S296   248'.48'41   75-44473

ISBN 0-687-22960-X

Verse quotation on page 38 is from the poem "Christ and We" by Annie
Johnson Flint, published by Evangelical Publishers.

MANUFACTURED BY THE PARTHENON PRESS
NASHVILLE, TENNESSEE, UNITED STATES OF AMERICA

To My Wife
JANE
Whose Love and Support
Makes It Happen!

Introduction

Recently I saw a poster of a tall lily blooming in silver glory, towering above a field of rubble and weeds.

So, too, this inspiring book by my friend Ernst Schmidt stands above the thousands of volumes that are published, like a white light of hope for troubled people.

The power of possibility-thinking is a dynamic force of Christianity that the author of this book understands very well. Every problem can be turned into an opportunity. Every obstacle is filled with possibilities. In this strong volume, the mind and heart of one of America's most successful pastors turns potential negatives into actual positives. Enemies become friends. Darkness is turned into light. Hope rises out of the ashes.

I was profoundly moved and strongly inspired by these chapters that read like beautiful poetry yet speak with the clarity and power of forthright command.

It is a joy to witness the launching of a book that you know will contribute to the solution of the greatest problem facing our country today—that of transforming people from negative thinkers to possibility thinkers.

I cannot imagine anyone reading this book from cover to cover and not experiencing a permanent change in his mind-set.

No person will be the same person after reading this book. The change may be of only slight degree, but a small degree of change makes all the difference in the world if you carry the line far enough!

To the sincere reader I say, "Be prepared to step into a new world. Get set for a better life. Be sure of this one thing:

MAKE IT HAPPEN!

problems are pregnant with great possibilities! This will be the great discovery as you learn to think of opportunities through this helpful ministry."

Robert H. Schuller
Garden Grove, California

Acknowledgments

One's first book is a thrilling, yet disturbing experience. I say to myself, "This is my book." Yet is it? Is it not a contribution of things read and heard—written and discussed? Is it not the impact of powerful people like J. Wallace Hamilton, Norman Vincent Peale, Robert Schuller, and others who have adventurously torn the Christian faith out of the stuffy closets of pietism and lifeless ritual? Is it not the fruit of the opportunities breathed into the life of a person by people who love him?

Surely a book is that and much more. I stand in profound gratitude to all who have given so freely to the great pool of ideas from which we all drink and in our own way try to contribute.

Specifically, my thanks and deep gratitude to Irene Harrell, whose creative genius enabled her to edit my work so that it flows and is easily read by young and old alike. To Audrey Quinn, my secretary, without whose dedicated persistence this book would never have been. To Beth McDowell, who read, corrected, and suggested ways in which the material could be best transferred from spoken to written word. To my family, Jane, Lynn, Mark, and Julie, who love and understand and fill life with boundless opportunities. Last, but not least, to the members of Gloria Dei Church, who throughout the years have ministered to me as it has been my joy to minister to them. To you, the reader, for whom opportunities knock every day; may you find the joy of letting them in.

Contents

Opportunities in
Adversities

There are no difficulties in life—
　only opportunities.
　　There are no disappointments in life—
　　　only opportunities.
　　　　There are no disasters in life—
　　　　　only opportunities.
　　　　　　There are no problems in life—
　　　　　　　only opportunities.
Do you believe that?
A woman came to me
　and opened her heart
　　to pour out her story
　　　through a veil of tears.
After I had listened for a long while,
　I said—
　　"You don't have a problem—
　　you have an opportunity."
Disappointment shadowed her face.
　She thought I was making light of a serious situation
　　or that I was crazy.
But I am convinced
　that every difficulty
　　every problem
　　　every disaster
　　　　every disappointment
　　　　　is a diamond mine—
　　　　　　if you are rightly related
　　　　　　　to Jesus Christ—
　　　　　　　　if you are open and receptive
　　　　　　　　　to his power in your life
　　　　　　　　　　to guide and direct you.

MAKE IT HAPPEN!

Life is a matter of perspective—
  of how you look at things.
The problem thinker
  is the guy who walks around saying—
    "It's never going to work.
      It's never going to come out right.
      It's never going to make sense.
      It's got me beat.
        I can't lick it."
When a guy feels that way,
  he's going nowhere but down.
The opportunity thinker
  is the person who feels pain
    sheds tears
      feels the props of life
        being ripped out from under him
          but goes on to ask—
            "What does this teach me?
              What is it saying to me?
                What new challenges
                  does it put on the horizons
                  of my life?
                What new doors will it open
                  to my tomorrows?"
Problem thinkers bury life.
  Opportunity thinkers unearth treasures.
You can see it in your own life.
Most of us are problem thinkers
  and when something goes wrong—
    Oh brother!
      Nothing else matters.
      We moan—
        "I got a raw deal.
          There's no tomorrow."
Ask yourself—
  "What is the worst thing
    that has ever happened to me?"
      Look back on all the grief and heartache
        you caused yourself and others
          as you dealt with that worst thing.

14

Ask yourself—
  "What would have happened
    if I had turned it over to the Lord?"
If you had,
  he'd have opened doors for you.
    He'd have put a sunrise
      on the horizon of your life.
        He'd have given you
          new opportunities.
            He'd have fulfilled your life
              in a new dimension—
                if—you had been receptive
                  to his guidance.
Most of us wallow
  in a lot of sentimental nonsense
    that suffocates and strangles.
A fellow told me he had broken up with his girl.
  He was really disturbed, saying—
    "I don't know what to do.
      She was everything to me—
        my whole life—
          the one and only girl
            in the whole world
              as far as I'm concerned."
Nonsense!
  For the opportunity thinker
    there are thousands of one and onlys
      out there.
        Not all at once,
          but they're there.
A woman lost her husband.
  She wrote on his tombstone—
    "The light of my life has gone out."
      Two years later
        she married another man.
        She said to the bishop—
          "I've got to change that tombstone."
          "No," he said
            "just add to it,
              'I struck another match.'"

MAKE IT HAPPEN!

The opportunity seeker's creed is:
  Life is for living!
    If it gets comfortable,
      I will not coast.
        If it becomes empty or dark,
          I will strike a new match of opportunity
          and with God's help
            move forward
              in its light.

Opportunities in
Blindness

Our tour bus was a bit late
  as it came down around the Mount of Olives
    from Bethany
      but we finally arrived
        at the beautiful Garden of Gethsemane
          filled with huge, gnarled olive trees.
Beside the garden
  is a church
    and we sensed that the monks
      who tended it
        wanted to hurry us through
          so they could have some lunch.
Nevertheless
  we went into the church and looked around
    in the darkness.
      There were a few flickering candles
        on the altar
          and pilgrims of all faiths and nationalities
          were there.
In the center of the church,
  in front of the altar,
    was the rock of agony
      where Jesus prayed
        on Holy Thursday.
"Come on
  it's time to go,"
    a monk was saying,
      when I heard the sound of a cane
        hitting the floor of the church.
An elderly gentleman
  was coming up the aisle,
    feeling his way along,
      and a young woman

was trying to describe the rock to him.
He was blind.
The old man set his cane aside and knelt,
first running his fingers over the rock's surface
then holding them still for a few moments.
At last
he bowed his head low
and kissed the rock.
Many months have passed
since I watched him
but I've not forgotten.
"That's what the rock is all about,"
I told myself.
"That rock is where
a blind man learns to see."
There are other kinds of blindness
besides physical blindness—
personality blindness
(when we look at ourselves
and fail to see
what is so obvious to everyone else)
directional blindness
(when we don't know where we're going
or what we're supposed to do).
Jesus had directional blindness
the night he stumbled into that garden
with a few friends
and threw himself down
on that rock.
He had no idea
what he wanted to do.
He could not comprehend
what was happening
and so he prayed.
He prayed so hard
and so intensely
that sweat came from his brow
as though it were blood.
There was agony.
There was confusion.

18

He cried out—
"Father
I don't know what you want me to do.
I sure don't want to die—
to face this thing alone.
Tell me what's right!
Help me!"
In that conflict
in that battle,
his blindness was removed
and after searching
wrestling
agonizing
about who he was
and what God wanted of him
he got up and said—
"It's time to go, friends.
I can't give this cup
to anyone else."
There was no confusion,
no anxiety,
only purpose
and certainty—
the miracle of prayer.
Prayer is not easy.
I find it hard at times.
Sometimes I don't know how to start.
Many times
when I pray
I sound empty
and the words bounce off the ceiling
as if there's no one listening.
Around our table at home
we have begun taking turns
at prayer.
How silly we sound to one another!
We find ourselves laughing sometimes
at the prayers we hear ourselves praying.
But over the months

                        this praying has taken on a new dimension
                            of reality.
Suddenly we are expressing ourselves more clearly,
    talking to God,
        listening . . .
            We can see that prayer brings growth.
Some say that prayer is a cop-out,
    an escape,
        a sign of insecurity
        or personal weakness.
Let them think that,
    but when you find yourself
        on a wavelength with the Master,
            when you come in contact with him
                and share what you feel and think and are,
            you'll have discovered one of the great foundations
            on which abundant life is built.
If you don't pray
    you'll miss the human confrontation
        with the divine,
            the place where a person finds direction,
                where blindness leaves
                and sight is given.
I wish I could have seen
    inside the old man who knelt and kissed the rock.
        I wish I could have known what happened to him.
But I do know what happened to Christ.
    He stood and said fearlessly—
        "The hour is at hand."
More things are accomplished by prayer
    than we can ever imagine.
        Blindness is an opportunity
            to pray
                and to see the will of God.

Opportunities in
Tension

"O God, am I uptight!"
  But God is trying to give us peace—
    not the kind that's here today and gone tomorrow,
    not the kind that's fragile,
      that shatters—
  he wants to give us a peace
    that gives substance
      strength
        and meaning to life.
I hear you saying
  deep in your heart—
    "Boy! I wish I had that!
      I wish that peace was mine!
        I wish I had a sure direction
          for my life!
    But the storms of life overwhelm me.
      I get nervous
        disjointed
          uptight.
            I come unglued."
When tension gets you,
  when you are twisted by it
    and it gnaws at you
      and turns you into something you don't like,
  what do you do about it?
One fellow says—
  "Oh boy! Am I tired!
    I think I'll go to bed
      and sleep for two months."
Another guy says—
  "I'm wound tighter

than an eight-day clock.
Give me three doubles."
A third fellow says—
"When I get tense
I get in the car
and drive for miles and miles.
I run away from everything."
What do you do about your tension?
You get rid of it immediately,
right?
You step on it
run from it
bury it
in pills
booze
anything.
But did you ever ask—
"Tension, what are you trying to say to me?"
Tension is part of an ordained cycle of God
trying to tell you
that something's out of whack,
something's wrong with your life,
something needs attention.
Tension is God's signal for
"CAUTION!
Take a new look at your life.
Take inventory of who you are
where you are
where you're headed."
Tension says—
"I want you to be yourself,
not a phony."
We were taught to be phonies.
Our parents told us—
"Don't argue.
Don't fight.
Be nice.
Be sweet.
Don't upset anybody.

                Keep calm.
                    Don't rock the boat."
We listened and we obeyed
   outwardly.
      But inwardly
         we churned.
We smiled
   outwardly.
      But inwardly
         we seethed—
            "Boy! I wish I had told so and so
               what I thought of him!"
            "What a lousy resolution we passed!
               Why didn't I stand up
                  and express my opinion?"
Try being yourself
   without being socially obnoxious.
      It's not as tough as you think.
         It makes you feel a lot better.
            It relieves the tension,
               keeps it from building up.
                  What's more important,
                     people know who you are
                        and where you're coming from
                           and that matters.
Tension says—
   "Keep things simple."
      Your problem has a simpler solution
         than the one you've concocted.
A man said—
   "For sixty-seven years
      I've worried about things
         that never happened."
That's the way most of us live—
   borrowing trouble.

Your teenager is out late—
   You wait
      get uptight
         start to steam.

MAKE IT HAPPEN!

You imagine—
    drunk—lost—in jail
        accident—hospital—morgue.
Then he walks in
    alive, in one piece,
        with a simple explanation.
You could kick yourself
    for being so stupid.
You could wring his neck
    for being so thoughtless.

Somebody telephones—
    "I've got to talk to you
        right away!"
            and slams the receiver.
You wait
    wondering—
        "What did I do?
            Is he mad?
                Bringing bad news?
                    Wanting to borrow some money?"
The doorbell rings.
    You jump out of your skin
        but it's nothing special;
            he just wanted to talk.
The doctor puts down his stethoscope
    clears his throat and says—
        "I have something to discuss with you."
You leap to conclusions—
    "Buy me a lot under a shade tree.
        Face me out of the wind.
            Six feet by three,
                I'm coming.
                    Life is over."
But all he wanted
    was to tell you about his new office hours.

Keep it simple.
    Stop making mountains out of molehills.
        Humans aren't designed to carry mountains.

Think of the good things:
    It takes less energy.
        It makes less tension.
            It keeps life fun
                instead of frantic.
Tension says—
    "Stay away from pessimistic,
        negative,
            undercutting people.
                Don't listen to them.
                Be positive!"
Paul Tournier wanted to write.
    He asked five friends to read his manuscript.
        They read it and tore it apart—
            "Paul, forget it.
                It's no good.
                    You don't have anything
                        worth saying."
They broke his spirit.
    He wanted to quit
        but his wife said—
            "No, Paul. Try."
He went to a publisher.
    "No thanks."
        He went to a second publisher.
            "I'm sorry.
                We can't use it."
                    He went to a third publisher.
                    "You bet—it will sell."
Best sellers flowed from his pen
    but pessimists almost kept them from happening.
When your kids come in with their dreams,
    don't be a no-no bird.
        Don't say—
            "Don't do this.
                Don't do that.
                    It'll never work.
                        It can't happen."
Help them chase their dreams!
    Encourage them to try!

MAKE IT HAPPEN!

Don't be an anchor—
be a sail!
Don't be a leaner—
be a lifter!
Life needs the direction
purpose
and meaning
you can give it.
Without them
life's dull
meaningless
lifeless.
Find something that stirs your heart,
that sends excitement singing
through your veins.
If you have a dream in your heart,
fulfill it!
If you have an aspiration in your spirit,
search it out!
If you have a hope,
open the gates!
If you have an ambition,
give it life!
Be creative with your tension.
Let it work for your good
and God's glory.
Everything God has given you has a purpose.
When you use tension creatively
you'll discover the gift—
PEACE—
not a peace that removes you from turmoil
but a peace that gives you strength—
a foundation on which to live
and build and move.
God is not far—
he's near
when you sit down
and take a look
at what he's trying to say to you.

Tension wounds
  but it can also heal.
    Tension destroys
      but it can lead to discovery.
        Tension fractures
          but it can bring you to wholeness.
Tension is God's gift—
  your opportunity
    to find the peace
      the world can't give
        or take away.

Opportunities in
Hard Times

Economic problems are upon us:
  If you go to a shopping center,
    you know it.
  If you go to a gas pump,
    you know it.
A cartoon in the newspaper
  showed a husband and wife
    coming out of the grocery store.
      She was carrying a little bag.
        He said—
          "Remember, honey,
            when it took two of us
              to carry twenty dollars' worth
                of groceries home?"
Things are changing.
Financial problems are real:
  the great campaigns fall short;
    agencies dependent on individual support
      are having difficulties—
        some of them are closing their doors.
The American people are asking—
  "What is tomorrow going to bring
    and can we afford it?"
The dollar is tight.
  That's not easy to live with—
    especially for us,
      who have been used to
        a different set of circumstances.
For the last thirty years
  there was no way to go but up.
    We've raised our children
      to think that all they had to do was ask
        and they would receive.

We gave.
    We provided
        liberally and freely.
We mortgaged ourselves to the hilt.
Now we have to tell these kids
    "No.
        We can't afford it.
            We can't do it.
                You can't have it."
In the past
    if we needed something,
        we would just go out and get it.
            If we didn't have the money
                to pay now,
                    we signed the installment agreement
                    to pay later.
It was very simple;
    but now our paper empires are coming apart.
        We can't do these things anymore.
            The budget can't handle it.
Across the nation
    people who have built their empires
        on a shaky structure of credit
            are manipulating their resources
                hocking their valuables
                    trying to keep their heads above water
                    trying to keep going
                        trying to stay solvent.
It becomes more and more difficult
    more and more degrading
    more and more intimidating.
We told our kids
    that a good education
        was the key to a good salary.
Young married couples
    believed that the key to happiness
        was owning a home
            a car
                and other *things.*

MAKE IT HAPPEN!

Middle-aged people
  predicated happiness
    on safe-deposit boxes big enough
      to store the treasures
        of their productive years.
Retired people
  said that happiness was money in the bank
    and security for their old age.
And all of us
  from one end of the spectrum to the other
    chased the proverbial golden ring,
      but now the ring is beginning to rust.
      The green of our securities
        is coming off in our hands.
What next?
  Disaster?
No.
  Listen:
    The difficulties in our economic situation
      are going to provide you and me
        with one of the greatest opportunities
          life has yet to offer.
If you see nothing but a drooping economy
  and a shrinking buck,
    you don't know what you're looking at.
In the midst of all the financial problems
  you and I have a peculiar opportunity—
    the same one the prodigal son had
      when he had spent everything.
When his money was gone
  he discovered there were things in this world
    that money couldn't buy.
When things got tight
  he began to take a look at himself
    and he found priorities far more essential
      than money could ever be—
        priorities like peace
          joy
            friends
              love.

It's always nice
   to have the things that money can buy.
     But it is much better
       and far more important
         to have the things that money cannot buy—
          things we generally overlook
          when we chase the golden ring.
We have conned ourselves into thinking
   that everything has a price tag on it.
We have concluded
   that we can solve all social ills with money.
I admit that lack of money
   lies at the root of some of our social problems
     but we have taken the fiscal approach
       and blown it completely out of proportion—
       into economic determinism.
We are convinced
   that if we want to get rid of slums,
     we need more money
   if we want better education for our children,
     we need more money
   if we want something done about mental illness,
     we need more money.
All of that is nonsense.
What we need is caring—
   a different attitude in our people.
Give people a new vision,
   new goals,
     and money automatically happens
       as the program grows.
We can spend millions and millions of dollars
   on hospitals
     police forces
       redevelopment authorities
        mental health centers
         special education
         churches—
but it's all down the drain
   without people to make it happen,
     people on fire with an idea,

MAKE IT HAPPEN!

    people dedicated to goals,
      people committed to things
        that money can't buy.
I won't insult your intelligence.
I know the value of money in our lives
  but I also know that once we've dedicated ourselves
    to pursuing *it*,
      we generally overlook
        the qualities it can't buy.
The economic crunch gives us
  an opportunity to look at ourselves
    to reevaluate our values.
When the prodigal son
  lost everything he thought was important,
    he took a look at himself.
      Penniless,
        he went home to his father
          where he found all the things
            that money can't buy—
              peace
               joy
                  friends
                  love.
Times like these
  give us a chance
    to look at ourselves,
      to figure out
        what we really want.
Look at the manger
  look at the cross
    look at the empty tomb
      and ask yourself—
        "Can money buy that
          with all of the joy
            and purpose
              and value of life
                it gives you?"
The prodigal discovered
  that what he thought was important
    had fallen through his fingers.

He went home to his father
  and he rediscovered there a treasure—
    love and joy and peace—
      the most precious things in life to him.
You see,
  don't you?
All it takes is an opportunity attitude.
  In a tough time
    God has given you and me
      a new chance
        to learn what really matters,
          to rediscover
            the greatest treasure of all.

Opportunities in
Risk

Risk anyone?
　No thanks.
We are slowly developing into a nation of people
　who are quite content
　　with taking such carefully calculated risks
　　　that they are not risks at all.
For the most part
　we would rather keep the status quo—
　　not rock the boat
　　　buy only blue chip stocks
　　　　drive only on well-marked highways
　　　　　not stick our necks out
　　　　　　and never get too far away
　　　　　　　from a telephone.
I turned on the TV
　and watched a program called "Going West."
Average
　ordinary
　　everyday people
　　　like you and me
　　　took wagons through the dense forest of the Alleghenies
　　　　and hacked out an area
　　　　　where they could make a dirt farm.
They forded rivers
　which even today take a stout boat.
　　They tried it with rafts
　　　and overloaded wagons
　　　　and the mortality rate was fierce.
They dragged their wagons over trails
　through cracks and crevasses of the Rocky Mountains,
　　discarding lifelong treasures

as they forged their way across the alkali deserts
    day after endless day
without even a chance to bury their dead.
    ' But they moved on.
People slouched in their easy chairs,
    glasses of beer in hand,
        watching the history of our great land unfold.
        People took another sip
            shook their heads and said—
                "I could never have done that."
And for the vast majority of us
    that's true.
        We could never have done that.
            We like to play it close to the vest.
                We don't want to go
                    where there is any chance of danger.
                We want our guarantees written out.
Me go to that place?
    Heavens no!
        There's too much danger
            too much risk.
                I won't get involved in that.
If you want to find the risk-takers in our society
    you have to look at those outside the law.
If a fellow decides to break into a Brink's armored truck,
    he plans and plans and plans
        and then he plans again.
            Finally he risks all
                to do the job.
If a group decides
    to steal a priceless art collection
        they scheme and plan,
            putting an unlimited amount of ingenuity
                into making sure
                    they can pull the robbery off.
                        And they risk everything to do it.
Those of us on this side of the law
    are far too content
        with taking just the necessary risks

>   for keeping body and soul together.
>   We say that's enough for us.
But think!
> Unwillingness to take risks
>   incapacitates us for living our lives
>   healthfully and fully,
>   makes us block
>   progress and growth.
We must reevaluate our stagnant
> no-risk philosophy.
>   We must change.
You may not change all the way
> from Hold That Line!
>   to
>   Charge!
>   but get your gears in motion
>   so that the next time you are in a position
>   to make some choices
>   you will make them with vision.
Look at Paul.
He wrote to the church at Corinth,
> a church he founded,
>   a church he loved,
>   a church he wanted to visit—
>   "I can't come to you yet
>   because I am going to stay here in Ephesus
>   where a great door of effective work
>   is opening up to me
>   and there are many adversaries."
Ephesus was a city
> where no Christian lived,
>   a city of superstition and immorality.
>   Ephesus was the center
>   of the worship of the goddess Diana.
Paul was going to stay
> in spite of the risks.
A Christian is a realist
> and a person of faith,
>   a person who sees that life must go on,
>   that challenges must be met

with intelligent planning
   and intelligent perspective,
      allowing risks to take place
         for the ultimate good.
The gospel of Jesus Christ was spread that way.
   If you and I have any conviction within our hearts
      that Christ undergirds
         the very structures of our lives,
            it is because somebody out there
               dared to risk
                  to make it real
                     for you and me today.
I know the church has great problems.
   The prophets of doom tell us
      that we are losing our effectiveness,
         that the power of Christ
            is no longer an effective tool in our society.
We've got all kinds of nit-pickers
   and rock-throwers
      who plink away at us
         always showing us how bad we are.
I know all that
   but two thousand years of history have shown us
      that civilizations have come and gone
         while the prophets of doom lifted their voices—
            just as they are doing today—
               to no effect.
The gospel of Jesus Christ remains.
   It is here
   and it is powerful.
If Christ means something to you,
   if the gospel is alive in you,
      you have to share it.
You say—
   "I can't talk to people about my religion."
Don't give me that.
   If you get a new carpet,
      you gab to the whole neighborhood about it.
         "Look what I've got!"

MAKE IT HAPPEN!

If you get a new car
　　that happens to work right
　　　for the first month or so,
　　　　you tell everybody—
　　　　　"Isn't it marvelous?
　　　　　　You ought to buy one like it!"
You can talk about anything you want
　　and when you are caught up
　　　with the gospel of Christ,
　　　　when you know
　　　　　he's the answer to your life,
　　　　　you can share that too.
Risk?
　　Yes, there will be risk involved.
　　　There will be those who laugh,
　　　　who call you "fanatic."
　　　　There will be those
　　　　　who poo-poo anything you do
　　　　　if you stick your neck out.
But there are new horizons
　　new frontiers
　　　and new adventures
　　　　for people who stand like Paul and say—
　　　　　"I see the door of effective work
　　　　　and I am not too hung up
　　　　　　on the great opposition
　　　　　　to risk it."
It boils down to believing what the poet says—
　　that with this tremendous treasure,
　　　the gospel of Jesus Christ,
　　　　the fact is—
　　　　　"Christ has no hands but our hands
　　　　　　to do his work today;
　　　　　He has no lips but our lips
　　　　　　to speed men on their way."
Christians have no choice
　　but to take the risks
　　　no matter what—
　　to seize the opportunity
　　　for great reward.

Opportunities in
"If Only . . ."

Have you ever run into someone
   you haven't seen for quite a while
      and after you've had a little conversation—
         gotten caught up to date with each other—
            he starts to walk away
               and you feel yourself saying—
                  "Boy! He's got it made!"
You begin to compare your own situation—
   the one you're stuck with—
      and soon you hop on a merry-go-round
         that has you chasing your tail,
            asking the inevitable questions:
               "If only I had what he has
                  wouldn't it be wonderful?
                If only I had his money
               her looks—
                  If only . . ."
Listen.
   The longer you ride
      on that if-only merry-go-round
         the more you find yourself
            chasing your own tail.
If only I were younger?
   You become old
      only when you stop wanting to grow.
         That can happen at fifteen
            as well as at ninety.
Anyone who thinks he is getting old
   just because he is moving along chronologically
      doesn't have a very good grip on life.
You don't become old
   just because someone rips a page off the calendar

and sings Happy Birthday to you.
　You get old
　　because of the way you see yourself.
Don't say—
　"If only I were younger
　　I'd set the world on fire."
　　It doesn't work that way.
　　　Some of the greatest things that happen
　　　　are *made* to happen
　　　　　by people with white hair on their heads
　　　　　and wrinkles on their faces.

If only I were thinner?
　"Look at me—
　　a fat, frumpy old tomato—
　　　I feel like I've been on Medicare
　　　for a thousand years."
　If you feel that way about yourself,
　　go to a doctor
　　　start on a diet
　　　　set your mind on changing your weight.
　Don't sit around feeling sorry for yourself
　　thinking up excuses,
　　　saying—
　　　　"Oh, I've always been fat.
　　　　I'll never be any different."
If only I looked better?
　We all think that sometimes.
　　We look at our physical deficiencies and say—
　　　"If only I didn't have this—
　　　think what I could do!"
　There are specialists
　　who can help you minimize your defects
　　and accent your positive qualities.
　　　If you're interested in improving
　　　　who and what you are,
　　　　　go to them.
　　　　　　Improve your assets.
　　　　　　Get on with living.

Don't sit around feeling sorry for yourself
  because you lack something
    you wish you had—
      instead, change your life.
When I was younger
  I saw my hairline
    slowly but surely
      creeping toward the collar
        at the back of my neck.
          I didn't like that.
            One day I screwed up my courage
            and went to somebody
            who showed me
              how to do a lot with a little.
            I did
              and I liked it.
Don't be unhappy
  with who and what you are.
    Make the best of what you've got.
    Get on with living.
      Don't be stuck with "If only . . ."
An opportunity seeker
  finds ways to capitalize on his deficiencies.
    He doesn't complain about what he lacks;
      he uses what he has
        and he doesn't worry
          about what people will say.
Look at Zaccheus,
  a fellow with money and power
    who buys himself slaves and
      makes an impact on the decision-making process
      of a very important city—
        a man of authority,
          a leader in his community.
Zaccheus was short—
  he was a shrimp.
    He wanted to see Jesus
      but he couldn't see over the crowd.
      Did he moan—
        "If only I were taller"?

MAKE IT HAPPEN!

Did he give up and go home?
No!
Zaccheus climbed a tree.
What would you have said
about a man of his station
climbing a tree on Main Street?
Zaccheus didn't give a tinker's damn
what all the busybodies on the street would say.
He couldn't care less.
He knew what he wanted
and he got it.
When Jesus came by
Zaccheus saw him.
What's more
Jesus saw Zaccheus
and reached out for him.
All Zaccheus had hoped for
was to get a look at Jesus
and lo and behold
here Jesus was coming to his house!
Our God always takes us higher
than we had thought of going.
He always takes us farther
than we had in mind.
You want a cozy little cottage,
comfortable and convenient,
with a bowl of apples on the table—
he builds a palace
fit for a king
and tells you it's yours.
You want a nice little job,
just enough to keep you going,
to keep you interested in life—
he gives you an occupation
that utterly consumes you.
You want to put easy limits
on where you'll go
and he says—
"No limits."

It's exciting to let go of the if-onlys
  and get caught up in this dimension of life.
Once you push if-only aside,
  God fills you with purpose.
    Once you stop fretting
      about what you don't have,
        God gives you more than you could ask.
    Once you stop worrying
      about what people will say,
        you'll have time to listen
          to what God says.
And he says—
  "If I am in you
    and you are in me,
      we will bring forth an abundant harvest.
        Great will be the fruit
          of this vine."
Salvation doesn't mean
  just going to heaven,
    being saved for the hereafter.
Salvation at its root
  means room
    freedom
      the excitement of living
        in the now.
Salvation means
  Zaccheus could take all the little barriers
    he had erected around his life
      and move them back and say—
        "There is no limit to what I can do."
That's what God does for people
  who get rid of their if-onlys
    and make themselves ready to move and think
      in an opportunity attitude.
Jesus *is* life—
  a life of overcoming the if-onlys.
What an exciting life
  awaits you
    when you go at it with the Master.

Opportunities in
Estrangement

Back in the time of Jesus,
　if someone told you that you had leprosy,
　　fear roared through you
　　　shaking every fiber of your being.
　　　　Panic struck
　　　　　at the very heart of your life.
There was no hope.
　There was nothing anyone could do for you.
　　They wouldn't even let you die
　　　close to those you loved.
　　　　The word *leprosy*
　　　　　radiated an unimaginable horror.
Look at the leper in Mark 1:40.
　Can you imagine him as a young boy
　　running with his buddies
　　　in the streets of his village
　　　playing games in the hills
　　　　bouncing a ball
　　　　　off the synagogue wall?
Can you envision him
　growing up and marrying the girl of his dreams,
　　his childhood sweetheart,
　learning a trade
　　settling down and making a home
　　　raising a family
　　　　loving his children
　　　　　wrestling with them
　　　　　　enjoying them
　　　　　　　loving his wife
　　　　　　　　and she loving him back?
Laughter would ring in their home.
　And then one day

as the fellow was outside washing up,
    getting ready for breakfast,
        he noticed a gray spot
            on his hand.
He scrubbed harder.
    It's got to come off!
    But it doesn't
        and horror runs through him.
            "My God!
        If this is what I think it is
            what am I going to do?
                Maybe it's not—"
                    But he knows it is.
For a whole week
    he sleeps with his hand under his pillow
        and every morning
            in the revealing light of dawn
                he holds up his hand
                    and looks
                        hoping—
But the spot isn't going away
    it's growing—
        getting larger.
            He has no choice.
                He can't endanger his children
                    or his wife.
He has to be declared unclean—
    to go into exile
        and live in caves with others
            who have the loathsome disease,
                who live on garbage,
                    the leavings of society.
He finds himself separated
    from everything he loves.
        If anyone comes close to him
            he has to shout—
                "Stay away!
                I'm unclean!
                    For God's sake
                        don't come any closer!"

MAKE IT HAPPEN!

That's the man
  hoping and praying
    that he can die mercifully and quickly.
      That's the man
        who ran up to Jesus.
That was a foolish thing to do.
  Any leper who came close to a healthy person
    was subjected to stoning.
      Anyone who killed a leper like that
        had to answer to no one.
        But this leper risked it.
He ran up and fell down in front of Jesus
  and groveled in the dirt.
    This filthy
      dirty
        twisted
          sick human being said—
            "Oh, Jesus
              if you want to
                you can help me."
And Jesus did a remarkable thing—
  He touched him.
Nowhere else in the Scriptures
  do we see this happening.
    Normally
      when Jesus dealt with a leper
        He told him to show himself to the priest
          and as the man went,
            he was cured.
But here
  Jesus didn't see a leper;
    he saw a dejected pathetic man,
      a broken miserable human being
        so hungry for human compassion
          understanding and caring
            that Jesus couldn't resist touching him
              to make him whole.
There's power in the human touch.
Have you ever had a friend come
  and pour out her heart to you?

The problems seem insurmountable
and you say to yourself—
"What's she telling me all that for?
There's nothing I can do.
I'm all chewed up inside
but I can't do a thing for her."
You try to think of something to say
but nothing comes
and finally
you just sort of reach out
and take her hand in yours.
That touch speaks volumes
and helps more
than all the good advice in the world.
Help your wife on with her coat
and gently squeeze her shoulder.
It tells her you love her
just as surely as if you had put it on a billboard
with letters three feet tall.
Walk in the dark with your little child
and feel her slip her hand in yours;
it speaks of love
trust
and confidence
like nothing else in this world.
There's simple magic
in the human touch.
Have a fight with your wife.
Let the words be hot
hard
cruel
and cutting.
Let them even have an element of truth in them.
And there you are
lying in bed
everything in you jeering—
"You jackass!
Reach over and touch her.
Tell her you're sorry.

MAKE IT HAPPEN!

Tell her life's too short to waste
with idiotic behavior."
Don't roll over and pretend to sleep
a pall of uneasiness
settling over your restless heart—
touch her!
Have a fight with your teen-aged daughter.
Again let hard things be said
enmity grow between you
your relationship drift apart.
Reach out and grab her
pull her close to you and say—
"I'm sorry about it all.
I didn't mean it.
There are things more important
than fussing."
Fall out with a friend
and then one day
you happen to meet him on the street.
Walk up to him
take him by the hand and say—
"Joe!
Gosh, I'm glad to see you!
I'm sorry for the differences we've had."
Don't turn your eyes away
and hope he doesn't see you.
Touch him!
To touch another human being
is at times the most difficult thing to do
but it's the most magnetic and powerful
vehicle of communication you have.
As I counsel people,
time and time again they say something like—
"I don't know what to do with my daughter.
She won't listen to me.
I can't communicate with her at all."
Sometimes I ask—
"When's the last time you took a walk with your daughter
and put your arm around her?

When's the last time you wrestled with your kid
  on the living room floor?
When's the last time your family held hands around the table
  as you said grace?"
You ask me—
  "Is that going to solve the problem?"
No,
  but it might help crack the shield
    you've built around yourself
      and allow the fresh water of communication
        to flow through your spirit.
I'm not talking about something superficial;
  I'm talking about something
    at the heart of the gospel of Jesus Christ:
      the significance of touch—
        one human being caring for another
        and showing it.
Ask yourself—
  "What good is my home without it?
    What good is my community without it?
    What good is my church without it?
    What good is the world
      if we don't share the magic of the human touch
      with one another?
    What good am I without it?"
When you see another
  to whom you can reach out
    because you know that caring is more than a word,
      you will know that estrangement
        is an opportunity
          for the touch
            that heals and reconciles.

Opportunities in
Weakness

Power intimidates us
  frightens us
    limits us
      controls us
        and even destroys us.
Someone says—
  "Are you kidding?
    I'm not afraid of power.
      The guys who are so important,
        who think they're so high and mighty—
          I'm as good as they are—
            better than most of them.
              They don't scare me."
Oh no?
  Assume you're driving down the highway,
    your mind absorbed with where you're going
      what you're doing.
        You're obeying the speed laws
        but all of a sudden
          your rearview mirror frames
          a state police car
          right behind you!
You look at your speedometer
  your mind races back—
    "Did I pass on the wrong side?
    Did I run a yellow light?
      Did I go through a stop sign?
      What's he chasing me for?"
Your mind whirls—
  you think he's after you—
    until he passes.
      By then you're traveling 35 miles an hour.

Power scares.
  Power scares us all.
Assume that you go to your mailbox
  and find an envelope
    that says Internal Revenue Service
      in the upper lefthand corner.
        "Lord, they've got me!
          What did I do wrong?
            I declared everything.
              There's been a terrible mistake."
You fumble as you tear open the envelope.
  They only want you to give a reference
    for a prospective employee.
Power scares
  but you and I barely ever ask ourselves
    What is power?
      Who is powerful?
The state policeman who threatens you today
  could be in the unemployment line tomorrow.
The internal revenue man who investigates you today
  could be investigated himself tomorrow.
The President of the United States
  with the power of this great nation at his fingertips
    might live like a recluse tomorrow
      on the beaches of the Pacific.
What is power?
  Is it so frightening and devastating
    if a person can have it today
      and tomorrow be a beggar on the highway of life?
Why is power always out there?
  Why do we always think about power
    as something someone else has?
Are you a powerful person?
  I can hear you answer—
    "Gosh no.
      I can do all kinds of things
        I have the potential for many others
          but powerful
            I'm not."

MAKE IT HAPPEN!

By denying your power
   you are indicating that the God who made you
      has sent you into the world poorly equipped.
      He has sent you up to home plate
         without a bat.
         He has sent you to cooking school
         without a stove.
            He has sent you into the arena
            of daily battle
               without a weapon.
  And that just isn't true.
God knows what your needs are
  what the future is going to hold
    where the tomorrows are going to lead you
     what things in life
      will overwhelm you.
  And he's given you the power
    to handle every one of them.
If you don't believe that,
  you don't believe that God is a loving father.
As parents,
  we try to equip our children
    with the tools they will need
      to face life.
Do you think God is less loving than we are?
Who puts the limitations on your life?
  You do.
    Who says it won't work?
      You do.
        And everytime you say it
         you put a fence around yourself.
Your own fence says—
  "This is as far as I can go.
    Beyond that
      there's nothing for me.
      I'm fenced in."
And you blame the world for it.
You say—
  "A lot of people put fences around my life.
    When I went to school

they tested us,
    told us what our aptitudes were.
        That was one fence.
Another guy gave me a test
    that determined my intelligence quotient.
        That was another fence in my life.
And all those other people around me—
    my bosses
        my parents
            my friends—
                they put fences around me too."
But I say to you—
  "Friend
    anyone can tell you you have limitations
        but unless you accept them
            they're not really there.
                They have nothing to do with you.
    As soon as you say—
        'They're right'—
            you put up the fence yourself
                and you're the only one
                    who can take it down."
All of us
  have a potential for power
    that we don't realize.
How do you think Zechariah felt
  when he and the prophet Haggai
    were given the awesome task
        of rebuilding Solomon's temple?
They didn't have Solomon's strength
  manpower
    wealth
        or anything else Solomon had.
All they had
  was a bunch of weak
    ragtag
        weary refugees
            who had just come back to their homeland
                after years in captivity.

MAKE IT HAPPEN!

Zechariah was completely beside himself—
  "How am I ever going to build God's temple
    with them?"
Then, in a dream
  God showed him a candelabra
    with seven delicate little flames.
      Beside the candelabra
        were two olive trees—
          trees of peace—
            supplying oil for the lamps.
          The lamps glowed
            with flames so delicate
              you could have snuffed them out
              with two fingers.
The prophet asked—
  "What on earth has that to do
  with the herculean task
    of rebuilding the temple?"
God said—
  "Zechariah, it has everything to do with it.
  True, the flame is delicate.
    True, the oil comes
      from a symbol of peace
  but Zechariah
    you are not going to rebuild my temple
      with your might or your power.
  You are going to rebuild it because of my Spirit.
    The Spirit will flow through you
      and the lives of your people
        to rekindle within them
          the flames of strength and commitment.
    Even though you are few and weak
      you will become strong because of my Spirit
      and the temple will be built."
God was right.
  The work was done.

Look at your own powerlessness
  your own feeling of "I can't."
    "I can't" thinking

suffocates,
strangles.
"I can't" is all lies.
It's not true at all.
What would you have bet
that Zechariah and his bunch
would have rebuilt
the great temple of Solomon?
I wouldn't have given you
a thousand to one odds.
What would you have bet
that the conglomeration of fishermen and loan sharks
farmers and prostitutes
Jesus attracted around himself
would go out and change the course of western civilization?
I wouldn't have put a buck on that bet.
But that would be because I was overlooking
the power of the Spirit of God
working within the lives of people
changing their direction
allowing them new insight
never letting them underestimate
what they can do.
Who am I to put a restriction
on what can happen
when God's power is working
in a person like you or me?
Don't overlook that power
in your children
your mate
your elderly citizens.
Don't restrict that power in yourself—
let it flow.
Don't be afraid that someone will laugh at you—
that you'll be ridiculed
for marching to a different drum.
Don't dam up the power
and become full of frustration,
a stagnant reservoir.

MAKE IT HAPPEN!

Open your heart to the Master.
　Say—
　　"Lord, use me."
　　　Become a real channel
　　　　through which his power flows.
Don't be afraid of the power
　out there in the world.
　　You have a greater power within you,
　　　an untapped source of energy.
"Not through power or might
　will you build my temple, Zechariah,
　　but you will build it
　　　because of my Spirit.
　　　　It will work through you
　　　　　even though you are few and weak."
That's God's promise
　to all his people
　　and it spells unlimited opportunity
　　　for *your* life
　　　　when you let his Spirit
　　　　　work through you.

Opportunities in
Pessimism

Pessimism starts early.
  My small daughter was holding
    a fistful
      of skinny pretzel sticks.
        "Can I have one?"
          her brother asked.
            "Sure, Mark," she said
            wanting to share.
        But he took two instead of one
        and she cried—
           "Mark took two pretzels
             and I don't have any left."
        There she stood,
          her grubby little hand
            too small to close
               over the abundance she had left.
Do you see lack
  or abundance?
    Is the glass half-full
      or half-empty?
        Do you see the hole
          or the doughnut?
Why are we so frightfully pessimistic?
  Is life only the difficulty,
    the hardship,
      or is it full of endless possibilities,
      enthusiasm,
        excitement?
You'll never see the possibilities
  unless you have an opportunity attitude.
An opportunity attitude
  tells you there are possibilities

MAKE IT HAPPEN!

in spite of the difficulties
and the failures
and even because of them.

Some months ago
a woman with marital problems
came to see me.
She was a nice enough lady
with an ordinary hairdo.
She wore a dress with great big flowers
over a too broad frame.
Her husband was running around
with an attractive younger woman.
"I can't possibly compete with her,"
she moaned.
The more she talked
the more convinced she was
that there was nothing she could do
to win him back.
She was ready to quit
and wanted to know the best way
of getting out of the marriage.
I looked at her and asked—
"What do you do for yourself?"
She said—
"Well, you know
I've got four kids and a house to take care of.
I'm a housewife and mother—
I chauffeur the kids around.
There isn't very much time for me
to do anything for myself."
I looked at her again and thought—
"Pull out all the stops.
No holds barred.
Shock her into fighting for her life."
"You know,"
I said,
"it's obvious you don't think much of yourself."
"What do you mean?"
she snapped back at me.

OPPORTUNITIES IN PESSIMISM

"Well, look at yourself—
  nothing attractive about your hair
    your dress is clean
      but it doesn't do a thing for you
        you're too fat—"
Before she could storm out of the office
  I got in another word.
    "Now wait a minute.
      Why did you let the romance and excitement
        go out of your life
          just because you see yourself
            as a mother and a housewife?
      You have the same power
        that won him in the first place,
          the same power any human being has
            who sees herself as someone of value,
              someone to be proud of.
      You have the power of the Spirit of God
        which can work in you
          and help you to become
            a fantastic person."
She looked at me—
  she didn't think much of me—
    and she walked out.
Months later
  my wife and I went to a dinner party.
    I looked across the room
      and did a double take—
        there she was!
        Brand new!
Her hair was beautifully done;
  her clothes were stylish
    from head to toe;
  she was three sizes smaller.
She came across the room smiling—
  "Dr. Schmidt
    I'd like for you to meet my husband.
      We've just returned from a trip to the Virgin Islands.
      We had a marvelous time."

MAKE IT HAPPEN!

He shook my hand,
  beaming,
    and when he turned to speak to another man
    she leaned over and whispered—
      "I found the power."
Her charge accounts
  might have been stretched a bit
    but her personhood
      was all put together.

The easiest way to defeat ourselves
  is to be convinced
    even before we get up to the plate
      that we couldn't possibly hit the ball of life
      with any success at all.
There's no faster way to erode confidence
  than to minimize our own potential.
We don't need pessimism;
  we need faith in ourselves
    and in the God who made us.
Let your pessimistic "I can't"
  become an optimistic "I can."
Nothing's hopeless
  nothing's impossible—
    not even yourself—
  once you let go of your pessimism,
    your self-built fences,
      and grab hold of an opportunity attitude
      that can turn a mess
        into a message of victory.
You, like Paul,
  can do all things through Christ,
    who strengthens you.
      With God on your side
        nothing on earth can beat you.
        The sky's the limit
          for opportunity seekers.

Opportunities in
Fear

When I look at myself and others,
  I seldom see fear.
    We sophisticates have trained ourselves
      not to show fear.
        We hide it
          bury it
            do everything possible
              to conceal it
      but everyone is afraid of something.
Think of your childhood—
  you were afraid of the dark
    afraid of going to school
      afraid you might get polio
        afraid to be separated from your family
          to go to summer camp for a week
        afraid your parents were going to die
          and leave you all alone in the world.
You were afraid you wouldn't make good grades in school
  afraid you might be sterile
    afraid your children might not be born healthy.
When you got older
  you were afraid you had wasted your life
    afraid that what you had committed yourself to
      was not so hot in the first place.
You were afraid you were going to die
  before you were ready.
    The list goes on
      ad infinitum.
Every one of us harbors fears
  within the depths of our spirits
    but if you show fear
      you're a sissy,
        so you keep a stiff upper lip.

MAKE IT HAPPEN!

You tell the whole wide world
   you're going to handle everything that comes along
     but in your heart of hearts
       you know you are frightened
       and you can't afford to be.
You listen to Franklin Roosevelt's old cornball—
   "We have nothing to fear
    but fear itself"
      and you try to eliminate fear from your life.
       You treat it like an enemy,
         try desperately to get rid of it,
           and rarely if ever succeed.
It's dumb to want to get rid of fear.
   Fear can help you
    live and grow.
I want my kids to be afraid of some things:
   I want them to be afraid
    to walk into the street
      without looking for oncoming cars.
   I want them to be afraid
    to put their hands on a hot coil
     on the stove.
   I want them to be afraid
    of stepping on rusty nails,
     of drinking cleaning fluid.
   I want them to be afraid
    of a hundred other things
     that could destroy their lives.
Fear doesn't have to be an enemy—
   it can be an ally.

In October and November
   the eastern shore of Maryland
    is full of Canadian geese.
     In some cornfields
       you can see tens of thousands of them
        moving like a blanket of feathers,
          stripping the fields of everything edible.
Watching that blanket
   of brown and grey and white

you might think
the geese had nothing on their minds
except their bellies,
but you'd be wrong.
Dead wrong.
Look more closely.
Here and there
among the thousands that are feeding
you can spot geese whose necks are erect,
whose eyes scan the skies,
searching the horizon.
These geese are the sentries—
part of every flock.
At the first sign of danger
they give warning
and there is an explosion of feathers
wings—and thundering noise.
The sky grows black.
Fear has saved the flock.
Observe a white-tailed deer.
He spends more time standing still
smelling
listening
watching
than anything else.
A buck
can spring out of his bed
and clear a six-foot fence
in a single bound
when he's frightened.
A lonely prairie dog
scurries out of his hole
and stares around
looking as if there's nothing on his mind
except having a great big ball in life
but he never goes far from his den.
He's always alert for a hawk in the sky
or for a coyote around the corner.
He remains vigilant
so he won't become

> someone else's breakfast.
> Fear saves him
> time after time.

It's no different with us.
Fear is a God-given emotion
  that calls our attention
    to something essential.
Have you ever realized
  that when fear builds and builds,
    when it gets to a point
      where it engulfs you
        ensnares you
          shackles you
            and wants to destroy you,
              you have two choices?
You can go off the deep end,
  be wrapped in and destroyed by your fear,
    or you can handle fear creatively
      and let it lead you to life,
        let it lead you to trust.
It works that way.

We were four hundred miles from the nearest road
  in the subarctic.
Our plane,
  a Beaver float plane,
    landed on the George River.
      The wind was blowing from the mountains.
We loaded our gear into the plane—
  probably overloaded it—
    with hunters
      trophies
        everything.
Our pilot began to take off
  going down the river
    but we were able to climb only twenty feet—
      twenty-five feet—
        and the pines bordering the river—
          sixty to eighty feet tall—
            were towering way above us.

Behind the trees
  the granite mountain
    made its way to the sky.
      Suddenly the pilot made a complete left turn
      and flew straight toward the mountain.
        "Hey, are you crazy?"
          one of the guys yelled.
            "You're going to kill us!
            Look at those trees!"
Our voices trailed off;
  our hands grew clammy.
    We were scared.
"Hey, fellows,"
  the pilot said.
    "Relax, will ya?
      I've flown six thousand hours
        as a bush pilot.
          We're fine."
That was all right for him to say
  but those trees kept coming
    and the mountain kept coming.
      But as we moved off the safety of the water
        the downdraft of the mountain—
          which was there all along—
            began to lift our plane.
Slowly but surely
  the pontoons brushed
    the tops of the pine trees
      and we ascended right over the top
        of that mountain
          and were on our way home.
When we were most frightened
  we could do nothing but trust.
    Life teaches us that.
God said through Isaiah—
  "Fear not
    for I am with you.
      Be not dismayed
        for I am your God.

MAKE IT HAPPEN!

        I will strengthen you
            and I will help you
                and I will uphold you
                    with my victorious right hand."
The life of Jesus says to us—
    "You're going to have suffering
        you're going to have heartache
            you're going to have tears
                you're going to have agony
                    you're going to have a cross, ·
                        but fear not.
                        I am with you.
                            I am your God.
                                My victory is yours."
I have visited in hospital rooms
    where patients have told me—
        "I'm afraid
            uneasy
                uptight,"
                    and we have talked about it
                        and prayed
                            that Christ would come into their lives
                                and meet their needs.
Day after day,
    time after time
        patients have said—
            "Pastor, it works.
            When you left,
                suddenly the fear was gone.
                    I put myself in the hand of God
                    and I knew
                        I was going to be all right."
Fear is the opportunity
    that leads you to trust.
        The next time fear grabs at your life,
            take the opportunity to ask yourself—
                "What is fear trying to say to me?"
            And then hear God answer
                over and over again—
                    "Fear not—for I am with you."

Opportunities in
Envy

When you think of John the Baptist
  do you see some kind of wild man
    dressed in animal skins
      running around the wilderness
        munching on locusts and wild honey?
He jumps up on a rock
  every once in a while
    to proclaim to everyone within earshot—
      "Repent.
        Repent and be saved?"
That kind of picture
  is completely inaccurate.
John was not the kind of man
  we see downtown on streetcorners,
    one of those promoters of salvation
      shouting out to you
        over their dog-eared Bibles
          that you ought to repent and be saved.
John was not like that at all.
  He was a unique person.
When John lived
  people were hungry for a messiah.
    They were eager to have somebody
      meet their needs,
        give them direction.
Today,
  people are still starving
    for someone to follow.
      They're following all kinds of messiahs:
        gurus
          Yogis
            transcendental meditators . . .

MAKE IT HAPPEN!

You name it
  someone follows it.
In America alone,
  there are two hundred self-acclaimed messiahs
    with large followings.
      People are clamoring after them
        trying to find answers to their lives.
        Our society has an insatiable hunger
          for somebody who can give us the answers.
So it was in John's time.
  Poverty
    enemy occupation
    and brutality
      were destroying the people.
  When they saw John
    they saw a light at the end of a dark tunnel.
      People responded to him
        because he was a man of power.
John had large numbers of disciples.
  Great crowds followed him.
    When word got out
      that he was to preach in the wilderness,
        people came out of villages
          and out of cities
            to hear him.
              Wherever he went
                he had influence,
                  magnetism.
                    People hung on his words.
When you have that kind of thing
  going for you
    it inflates your ego
      your sense of self-satisfaction.
John was a central figure
  in the lives of thousands of people
    when someone else came along
      and superseded him.
        How did John react?
        He said—

"I must decrease
and he must increase."
That kind of self-abasement,
   self-control,
      is absolutely baffling
         to a fellow like me.
Everyone knows that someday
   somebody's going to come
      from behind you
   and he's going to be king of the mountain,
      the new herd bull,
         the new lion in the pride.
   He's going to be the new fellow
      who exceeds you
         in doing the job
            for which you think you're so indispensable.
Everybody knows that there's somebody
   somewhere
      who's going to do that
         someday.
But isn't it always going to happen
   sometime later—
      to a lot of other people
         before it ever happens to us?
When it happens to other people,
   it's all right.
      It happens all the time.
One day I watched the Dallas Cowboys
   play the Washington Redskins.
      For years Roger Staubach had been the quarterback
         of this legendary football machine—
            an unquestioned powerhouse.
The accolades of the crowd
   rang in his ears
      Sunday after Sunday
         for his performance and leadership.
            But one particular Sunday
               he was part of a losing effort.
               What's more,
                  he was injured.

MAKE IT HAPPEN!

Off the bench came a guy
   by the name of Longly
      that nobody had ever heard of.
         Longly took the reins in his hands
            and began to turn the game around.
               He won the game
                  with the most spectacular pro football
                     I had ever seen.
The crowds roared.
   A new champion had emerged for that day.
      And just as suddenly
         everybody was saying—
            "Roger who?"
That's what happened to John the Baptist.
   His followers started to drift away
      and pretty soon
         his disciples became upset—
            "John, what's happening to us?
               Look at what's going on!
               If this keeps up
                  we won't have *anything* left.
               Why is everybody following
                  this guy from Nazareth?
                     Who is he anyway?"
But John said—
   "I must decrease
      and he must increase."
         John was unique,
            actually *glad* for someone to be superseding him!
            There was no envy in him
               no jealousy.
                  John cheered Jesus on!
How do you fit that in?
   It isn't natural.
When you hear of a man who has succeeded
   in an area in which you have been trying to succeed
      for a long time,
         how do you react?
            How genuine is your joy?

70

Years ago,
   my wife and I went to visit an establishment
      built by a classmate of mine.
         He had really hit it big.
I did all the things
   that everybody else does
      when they're pretending to be happy
         for somebody else.
I said—
   "Hello!
      Congratulations!"
         and I was smiling a mile wide
            and all that kind of mishmash
               trying to cover up the hurt inside me.
On the way home
   I confessed to Jane—
      "Honey, I don't like how I feel.
         Why wasn't I the one to make it big?
         Why did I take the job I've got?
         We could have done what he did.
           We could have had what he has.
              The same opportunities were there for us.
              They could have been ours."
When we look at success,
   our viewpoint is invariably tainted
      with envy and jealousy.
Our children are about the only people
   for whom we can be genuinely happy
      when their star shines brighter than ours.
      We cheer them on
         with great love
         and hopes
         and dreams.
But let it be somebody else
   and it becomes tough to take.
      But John wasn't like that.
         He didn't have that jealousy,
           that green-eyed envy
              in him.

71

MAKE IT HAPPEN!

How do we go about getting
  some of John's peace
    into our personalities
      so that our envy will diminish,
        so that jealousy won't be twisting at us,
        so that we can exuberantly
          share the joy of others
            openly and honestly?
The key that will open the treasure house
  to John's kind of personality
    and character
      is prayer.
Don't shut me off.
  Don't tell me that's just preacher talk.
    It works!
How could you have envy
  jealousy
    antagonism
      or resentment
        for anyone
          whom you regularly bring before God
          in your prayers?
Ask God to give him guidance and strength
  in the very areas that awaken envy and jealousy
    in you.
Do it!
  You will have an enrichment of your spirit
    and a fulfillment of your character
      you never dreamed possible.
Envy recognized and confessed
  is an opportunity
    to pray and receive
      love and joy!

Opportunities in
Doubt

John the Baptist
  was in prison.
    He called his disciples to him
      and said—
        "Go to this Jesus and ask him—
          'Are you the one who is to come
            or shall I look for another?'"
John was becoming uncertain.
  He had doubts.
    Doubt destroys.
What is worse than a parent who doubts his child
  or a husband who doubts his wife
  or a wife who doubts her husband
  or a teacher who looks around her class
    and makes the kids feel she doubts their ability,
      their character,
  or an employer who looks at his workmen
    and obviously doubts their capacity
      to do the job?
Once you begin to doubt
  or to be doubted
    you'll soon be crying—
      "I don't know *what* to believe anymore!"
John had been so sure Jesus was the one.
  That's why he had said—
    "I must decrease
      and he must increase."
But now
  in prison
    with time on his hands
  he was walking in circles
    asking himself questions.
      All his former certainty had vanished.

MAKE IT HAPPEN!

We are like John—
  sometimes our faith is real and clear,
    sometimes we simply aren't sure.
We look around the world and see
  suffering
    heartache
      war
        and disaster.
We see
  famine
    injustice
      insensitivity
        loneliness
          lovelessness
  and we cry—
    "O God
      I want to believe
        but I don't see you anywhere.
          How do I find you
            in a world like this?"
Christ gives us an answer
  that is clear but unusual—
    the same answer he gave to John.
He says—
  "You're looking in the wrong place.
    You'll find me healing the lame,
      opening the eyes of the blind,
        the ears of the deaf,
      preaching the good news
        to the poor.
"You'll find me in those areas of life
  where I must be what I am
    and happy is the man
      who allows me to be
        what I am."
Christ made clear to John,
  as he must for us,
    that God does not exist for us;
      we exist for him.

God is what he is.
   He is not what you and I want to make him.
You can't mold God into a puny little concept
   and say—
      "This is what he is.
         This is how he acts.
            This is what he asks us to do."
Some people think they have God
   in their hip pockets.
      They walk around and tell you
         when to do something,
            how to do something
               to have God jumping through a bunch of hoops.
      They tell you exactly how you're going to march
         through the Pearly Gates.
Nonsense.
No box of brains can contain
   the majesty and mystery of God
      and make him perform
         like a trained seal.
Jesus says—
   "You won't find me in the great winds
      that sweep across civilization.
   You won't find me in the tremors
      that shake social structures.
   You won't find me in a book
      that's bound with leather.
   You won't find me entombed
      in ecclesiastical superstructures.
   You won't find me ensnared
      in theological concepts.
   But you will find me where love is.
      You'll find me where there is
         the still small voice of caring,
            where there is concern
               and the laughter that lifts human hearts.
               You'll find me where life grows.
I didn't come to you
   in a palace as you expected.
      I came in a barn.

MAKE IT HAPPEN!

I didn't walk the streets
  and through the arch of triumph
    carrying the baton of a victor,
      my ears ringing
        with the accolades of people.
I was dragged through the side door
  of a city wall
    with the spit of shame
      running down my face,
    with the blood of agony
      caking my eyes shut,
    with hatred and prejudice
      ringing in my ears.
Happy is the man
  who sees me for what I am.
    Look in the right places
      and you'll see me."
Doubt is an opportunity
  for you to cry out—
    "O God
      I want to believe you.
        Help me when I doubt."
And he will
  I promise you he will.

Opportunities in
Insecurity

Self-confidence
  is something few people have.
    It helps you stand taller
      and a little straighter.
        It gives you a lot of joy
          in the business of living.
Are you confident?
  "Me, confident?
    No way!
      I've got about as much confidence
        as a mouse at a cat show.
      I get upset
        about all kinds of things.
      I wish I *could* be confident."
We lose self-confidence
  at an early age
    in so many ways.
As individuals
  we're beautifully programmed
    to be vicious destroyers
      of confidence in those about us.
A father sets standards
  that intimidate his children.
    A kid does something stupid
      without thinking it through
        and I hear myself yelling—
          without thinking it through—
            "You dummy!
              How stupid can you get?"
Too late
  I want to cut my tongue out.

MAKE IT HAPPEN!

I'm only trying to help the kid—
 lift him to a new set of values,
  give him a better insight,
   let him see a more excellent way;
 but I'm not helping
  when I blunder out
   an insulting
    impetuous
     emotional statement
      like that.
I'm literally tearing down the ladder
 of self-confidence
  he tried so hard to climb.

A teacher destroys self-confidence
 when she takes a little one
  to the front of the class
  and berates him
   for not doing something
    he ought to have done.
A husband destroys self-confidence
 when he looks at his wife
  and calls her a "cluck"
   like he means it.

A boss
 wrecks your self-confidence
  when he tears you down
   in front of the whole office.
The boss's self-confidence vanishes
 when after he has climbed the ladder of success,
  he suddenly finds himself
   where the air is thin—
    his rightness challenged,
     his decisions questioned.
He feels the whole thing tremble
 beneath him,
  hears the baying of the hounds
   that want his job for themselves,
   feels them breathing down his neck.

Self-confidence is a rare quality today.
  More people than not don't have it
    but the way to get it is so simple:
      Give it to someone else—
        bolster his ego—
          and it comes back
            and bolsters you.
"Do unto others."
  It works every time
    but we forget that.
      We become insensitive to it.
Your little tyke
  does some fingerpainting
    (unbeknownst to you
      until she comes in laughing,
        paint running off the paper,
          dripping onto the floor).
"Look, Mommy!"
  But you don't see the painting.
    You see the floor
      and shout—
        "Just look at the mess you're making!
          Bring that thing here.
            Put it down.
              Just *look* at yourself!"
BOOM!
  That quick
    you've done it—
      wiped out her pride,
        deliberately and viciously squashed
          all her self-confidence.
She wasn't thinking about floors.
  She hoped you would appreciate the picture
    she painted just for you.
You acted like
  the floor was more important to you
    than she is.
Next time
  try—
    "Oh, what a beautiful picture!

MAKE IT HAPPEN!

Did you really paint it just for me?"
  and give her a hug.
You'll get big dividends
  that will set your heart dancing—
    hers, too.
Confidence is worth having;
  security is important.
Seize every opportunity
  to impart both to others.
    They will automatically
      come back to you.

Opportunities in
Opposition

Great opposition?
  Great opportunity!
    It sounds paradoxical
      but it's true.
        You will never have great opportunities
        without great opposition.
You don't like that idea
  and neither do I.
    If we want something done
      we want it done as nicely as possible,
        in a harmonious atmosphere.
We don't want opposition.
  We try to get rid of it
    as quickly as we can
      because opposition
        destroys opportunity—
          or does it?
You can't have both—
  or can you?
Businessmen say
  that the most difficult time
    in a business occurs
      when a competitor is breathing down your neck—
        upstaging you with better advertising,
          getting his product on the market
            ahead of yours.
Businessmen say
  opportunity is when things are going well—
    clients are plentiful
      and the orders are rolling in.
Right?
  WRONG!
    DEAD WRONG!

MAKE IT HAPPEN!

No business ever thrives so well
  as when its competitors
    are breathing down its neck.
      No business ever functions better
        than when it knows
          it has to keep on its toes
            to stay alive.
No government ever had greater opportunity
  than ours in the past few years
    when our young people were rioting in the streets,
      throwing their combat medals
        on the White House lawn.
When we heard screams
  and saw tears
  and blood
    as police dragged the kids
      one way or another,
        everybody started to wail—
        "My God!
            What is this country coming to?"
Instead of throwing everyone a bone
  our politicians should have seized the opportunity
    to take these youths
    and involve them
      in the complex of this republic,
        to give them an opportunity
          to develop zeal for this great land.

Take marriage.
  People say
    you can't have opportunity in an atmosphere of turmoil—
      where people are struggling with each other
        confronting one another
          challenging each other
            trying to discover
              who and what they are
                and where they stand—
      where accusations lead to tears
        and tears to insults

  and you find yourself screaming—
   "Why did I ever get into this mess?"
People say there can be no opportunity in that.
People say·
 opportunity is where we live together harmoniously
  even though we pass each other
   like two ships in the night.
 Opportunity is where there is tranquillity
  and relative peace,
   where we say to the whole world—
    "We have a happy marriage.
     Life is good."
Are people right?
 WRONG!
  DEAD WRONG!
No marriage ever has it so good
 as when two individuals are in conflict with each other—
  struggling for identity
   struggling to interpret their individual rights
    and their collective union
  trying to make
   the tremendous miracle of marriage take place
   in which two become one.
There is opportunity in that.
How often have you heard—
 "I had such a happy, peaceful home.
  Everything was going so well.
   I had no idea he was running around"?

The church is no different.
 Where there is debate and confrontation
  bickering and fighting
   disagreement and dissension
    and the prophets of doom wail
     that the church is coming to an end,
      nobody sees opportunity in that at all.
They think opportunity exists
 when you have an organization
  in which there is no dissension or aggravation,
   everybody walking harmoniously hand in hand

MAKE IT HAPPEN!

    with the Lord and each other
      straight to the Promised Land.
       Then things will work.
        Then there is opportunity.
Right?
  WRONG!
   DEAD WRONG!
Preachers show fantastic weakness here.
  We break our backs
    trying to please everybody.
  We can't get anybody mad at us—
    that would be wrong.
  We can't say anything offensive.
    We can't challenge anyone.
      After all,
        how could you have a successful church
          if people were mad at you?
  "Just make sure you love me"
    is the goal of some preachers.
Years ago,
  there was a guy out to get me.
    He looked for my weak spots,
      my Achilles' heel.
        He showed up at every meeting
          to drive his wedge between me and the people
          in whatever the situation happened to be.
I couldn't understand why
  but just knowing that he was going to be there
    made me work harder,
      made me sharper,
      made me do my homework.
I am a better minister today
  than I would have been without him.
    It's like the fellow who was asked—
      "What's the secret of your success?"
      He answered—
        "I had a great enemy."
In opposition
  there is opportunity
    to grow stronger.

Opportunities in
Disappointment

Jesus Christ
  is the greatest opportunity thinker
    of all time.
Once he was tired,
  bone-weary.
    He'd had a busy time
      and even his disciples were exhausted.
"Let's get away from here for a few days,"
  he said.
    "Let's get away by ourselves and rest.
    Let's forget the world."
They crossed the Sea of Galilee
  but when they got to the other side,
    they found five thousand people
      waiting for them—
        all of them hungry.
          But there was no food to feed them.
The disciples were disappointed—
  there would be no rest—
    and they said—
      "How are we going to find the means
        to feed all these people?
          Where could we find a baker
            with that much bread?
              Let's get rid of this crowd.
                We need some time for ourselves."
But Jesus saw them
  as sheep without a shepherd,
    and he took the difficult situation,
      the disappointment,
        and made the best of it.

MAKE IT HAPPEN!

We are like the disciples;
  we get to the point where we say—
    "Everybody's pulling at me.
      I have no time for myself.
        Tell them I'm not at home.
          Tell them I'm out.
            Tell them to go away."
If you're caught up in the people business—
  a doctor
    lawyer
      nurse
        mother
          father
            clergyman
              or a businessman—
  there comes a time
    when you see nothing
      but people pushing at you—
        asking
          complaining
          demanding.
They don't care
  about your private life.
    It doesn't occur to them
      that there might be fifty other people
      waiting in line
        for what you can give them.
    They all want
      what they want
        when they want it.
    That's all that matters to them.
You can look at these people
  and get irritated with them.
    You can cut them off
      shut your heart to them
        turn your back on them
        and justifiably say—
          "Look.
              I can't solve the problems of the world.
              I can't be everything to everyone

OPPORTUNITIES IN DISAPPOINTMENT

in my family,
in my profession.
There's got to be time for me!"
If you have planned for weeks
maybe months
to take some time off,
to go on vacation,
and suddenly something happens
and you can't go,
that really burns you.
You feel put upon,
sorry for yourself,
miserable.
You growl,
you grouch over the disappointment.
It chews you up inside.
It's hard to be the kind of person
who has understanding and compassion
in the midst of disappointment
or when interruptions interfere
with your heart's desire.
It's very trying
to have your plans fall apart.
But Jesus didn't react as we would have.
He responded with an opportunity attitude.
"What do you have?"
he asked.
When he learned there were only five loaves and two fishes,
he didn't negate what was available to him.
He didn't put it down
or say it wasn't worth anything.
He thanked God for it
and it became more than enough
to feed the five thousand.
If you have only five loaves and two fishes
in the face of an overwhelming multitude
you can give them to the Master and say—
"Take what I have
and give me the strength and courage
to use it wisely."

MAKE IT HAPPEN!

When you do that,
   he multiplies your offering
      to the point where you have five baskets
         full of leftover fragments.
But you've got to believe in what you have
   and stop worrying
      about what you lack.
Time and time again
   Jesus Christ multiplied things.
      And he still does.
They gave him a cross
   and he multiplied it from a symbol of death and sorrow
      into a symbol of victory and hope.
         They gave him five loaves and two fish
            and the multitudes were satisfied.
               Give him your life
                  and he'll multiply it
                     with power and love and strength.
When we are in Christ
   every problem
      every frustration
         every disappointment
            every lack
               is a wide-open door
                 of opportunity.

Opportunities in
Hopelessness

Someone you love
  is hopelessly ill—
    your child, perhaps.
A tidal wave of emotion
  floods over you.
You're devastated
  eroded
    destroyed.
      You cry out—
        "God, why?
          He's so young
            he has so much to live for,
              so much ahead of him.
          Why, God? Why?"
Futility answers mockingly—
  "What's the use?
    Nothing matters.
      Life has no meaning.
        It's all a lousy joke.
          We're all victims
            of fateful accident.
          Everything's hopeless."
But tell me—
  When is it really hopeless?
I see mothers
  bringing children to our cerebral palsy center—
    severely handicapped kids:
      they can't walk
      they can't talk
      they can't smile
      they can't feed themselves

they can't even hold their heads up.
One boy was sixteen years old
and weighed twenty-nine pounds!
But the mothers are not hopeless.
Each mother has a dream in her heart
believes there *is* hope
that something can be done,
and they are right.
Something *is* done.
Children walk
who haven't walked before.
Children sit alone
and hold their heads up.
Children with blank faces
begin to smile.
One little girl
shocks a staff member
almost out of his skin.
"No way, man"
the little girl says.
She has never spoken before.
"Come on," you say,
"you're just trying to make the best
of a raw deal."
No, you're wrong.
These people have hope—
a tenacious
vibrant
unbending hope—
a hope that will carry them
beyond whatever is in their tomorrows.
Why are most of us so quick
to get rid of hope
when storm clouds come?
A man learns that he has cancer.
"Oh, my God!
I'm going to die."
A woman feels a lump in her breast.
"Oh! I know what that is.
It's the end."

You discover Junior has smoked pot.
  Right away
    your imagination leaps
      to a hundred-dollar-a-day habit.
How you look at things
  makes a difference
    in what you do
      how you do it
        and what the future holds.
Victory is yours
  no matter what—
    if you have an opportunity attitude.
Now don't get me wrong.
  I'm not saying
    that an opportunity attitude
      turns mountains into molehills
      or clouds into sunshine.
But an opportunity attitude lets you see
  that what you think is hopeless
    isn't hopeless,
  that the insurmountable
    can be overcome,
  that there is always a way,
    always an answer.
Consider this biblical woman.
  Her daughter was desperately ill
    and she was looking for help from anyone.
      She even came to Jesus
        although she was a Canaanite
          and her people were hated by the Jews.
She told Jesus her problem
  and he didn't answer.
"Send her away,"
  the disciples said,
    but she wasn't defeated.
She knelt down in front of Jesus
  imploring—
    "I need your help!"
Jesus answered—
  "It isn't right

for me to take the children's bread
    and give it to dogs."
She knew what he meant—
  the Israelites were God's children,
    his chosen people.
  She was a Canaanite—
    her people were considered dogs and outcasts.
What would you have done
  in the face of an answer like that?
I'd have lowered my head and slunk away
   or my ego would have inflated like a zeppelin
    and I'd have given him some choice words
      that shouldn't be in a clergyman's vocabulary.
  Then I'd have stalked away
    muttering—
      "Who does he think he is
        talking to me that way?"
I would have kept my pride intact
  but I would not have won.
    I would have lost the very thing I wanted most—
      the healing of my child.
I would have been a quitter,
  given up my goal,
    let my pride and ego
      get in the way of my hope.
        I would have lost.
But not her.
  She said—
    "I want something that's bigger than my pride.
      You can hurt my pride, Lord.
        That's all right.
      But, Lord
        even the dogs
          eat the crumbs
            that fall from their master's table.
      Please, Lord
        give me a crumb—
          that's all I want."
She won the case.
  Her daughter was healed.

Look at the woman:
  Her opportunity attitude was fortified
    with the persistence of hope.
Most of us lack persistence.
  Oh, we start off with high hopes
    and great ideals
      but when the road gets rocky
        and bumpy
          we stop to reconsider—
            "Do I really want to pay the price
              for what I'm after?"
"No," we tell ourselves
  nine times out of ten,
    and we head for home.
      It's comfortable there
        and we're used to our hopelessness.
But the Canaanite woman pressed on.
  She wasn't about to give up.
    She wouldn't allow anything
      or anybody
        to deter her
          from making her request.
Was she scared?
  Probably.
    I bet her knees trembled
      and butterflies flew around inside her stomach;
    but that didn't stop her.
      Nothing did.
        And she got what she came for.
Friend, if there's something you want
  and you will persist with hope in going after it,
    you can get it.
There may be detours
  and roadblocks
    but there is nothing you can't get
      if you have an opportunity attitude,
        if you set your pride and ego aside
        and keep your eye on the goal.
No matter who you are
  or what you are

MAKE IT HAPPEN!

   or where you are
      or what you want,
   you can get it.

The Canaanite woman
   believed the person she was asking
      to do the thing
         could do it.
            She believed in God.
If you believe in a god
   who throws the stars and planets in the sky,
      who gives beauty to this world,
         who takes the dust of the earth
            and breathes human life into it,
   is there anything hopeless?
      Is there anything that can defeat you?
I don't care where you are—
   if life has led you to the mountaintops
      where the fresh breeze of success
         blows in your face
            and the world lies at your feet
   or if you're standing beside a grave
      of disappointment and sorrow—
wherever you are
   there is nothing to limit
      what the power of God
         can do in your life.
Believe that.
   Be persistent.
      Nothing can beat you.
Opportunity seekers
   are people who discover
      the mysteries of the kingdom of God.
Every opportunity—
   even hopelessness—
      has a golden knob
         just waiting for a person
            with the right attitude
               to turn it.
Maybe the right person is you.

Opportunities in
Death

Imagine what it might have been like
  to live before Easter happened.
    People were born into royalty
      and had the comforts and luxuries of life.
    People were born into the working class—
      a tolerable situation
        but not as comfortable as royalty.
    People were born slaves—
      always under the whip
        of some overlord,
      trained like a bunch of poodles
      to jump through hoops.
But no matter who they were—
  no matter what their station in life—
    people developed a workable philosophy:
    You are born
      you live
        and then you die.
    That was all—
      very simple
        very pragmatic—
          and they made the best of it.
        When you were dead,
        you were dead.
But then came Easter.
  Easter changed things.
On Easter
  a woman knelt in a garden
    crying.
      Her heart was broken.
  Heavy with sorrow,
    she spoke a name

        precious to her,
      throwing it to the winds
      calling—
         "Jesus, my Jesus
           why did you have to die?
             Why did the pall of death
               have to silence your name?"
For an answer,
  sneering death
    threw icy barbs of silence
      into Mary's heart.
Mary tried again
  to throw that name
    into the silent face of death.
      "Jesus,
        my Jesus."
And this time
  that name was caught!
Out of the misty dawn came a voice saying—
  "Mary."
And that one earthshaking word
  changed the course of human history.
No longer could anyone be satisfied
  with a simple life and death philosophy.
    No longer could anyone claim
      that he had a right to do just as he chose.
        No longer could anyone say with certainty
          that life ended in the grave
            and there was no more.
A name had been spoken
  and caught,
    piercing the dawn.
      Mary ran from the tomb
        filled with fear
          and filled with joy.
That's the way it has been
  ever since—
    fear and joy,
      belief and doubt,
        confusion and conviction.

The choirs sing—
  "The Heavens Are Telling the Glory of God."
Man has always used creation
  as the pinnacle of proof
    that God exists.
When the most sophisticated scientists
  see the structure—
    the intricacy,
      the intimacy,
        the interdependence in creation—
  they agree
    there had to be an Enabler,
    a Creator,
      a Force
        to pull it all together.
But when our faith also says that this same God
  gives man the power
  of resurrection
  some cry out—
    "Wait a minute!
    That's ridiculous.
      When you're dead you're dead.
      How can I believe that God
        will raise somebody from the dead?"
I answer—
  "What good is God
    if he can make a world such as this
    and then allow the grave
      to have the final word
        on the object of his love?"
I've stood at too many graves
  of people who believed in the Christ
    who lived,
      who found excitement in moving ahead
      and discovering
        the great opportunities of life.
        That was all there
          but somehow death cut it short.
Am I supposed to believe
  that death is the final victor over them—

that God's will is frustrated
and can never be completed in them?
If that's the case,
who needs God?
Don't talk to me about a god
who throws galaxies into orbit,
who juggles planets before breakfast,
if the grave can say to him—
"The very thing you love most
is ultimately mine."
Where is his sovereignty?
Where is his lordship?
Easter brings us to an empty tomb—
it tells us he is here.
He answers when you call his name.
He has become the victor.
If I can believe
that God made this magnificent world—
and I can—
then I can also believe
that resurrection is in his power
and his plan
and is a part of his people's lives.
Because of him
Easter happened
but we don't always act like we believe that.
Haven't you heard us say at funerals—
"Isn't it a shame he died so soon?
Isn't it a shame that Mary is dead?"
We say that
even though a fellow lived for ninety years.
It doesn't make any difference how old he was
we say—
"Isn't it a shame that he died?"
In spite of what we claim to believe
we look at death
as a final voice
that clamps the lid on everything,
that makes an end to it.

If you think like that
  death mocks you.
    Death stands there
      looking at you and saying—
  "Go right ahead—
    dream
      build
        try—
  It doesn't matter, dummy.
    It all comes to me
      in the end.
        I will put the lid on it.
          I will have the last word.
          I will hold everything
            in my grasp."
But Easter proclaims again—
  "No!
    God's will
      will not be thwarted.
        God will have his way.
          He didn't let it end on Calvary.
          He tore open the grave
            and let Christ come forth.
          His lordship and sovereignty
            are still above all!"
Throw back your head with me
  look at death and say—
    "Okay.
      I will go on loving
        growing
          caring
            dreaming
              being.
    And death,
      when you come,
        I will know it doesn't end with you
          because God has the victory.
          He raised up Christ
            and there is an Easter—
          the opportunity for eternal life!"

Opportunities in
Problems

A fellow came into my office
   and said—
      "Boy, do I have problems!"
   I replied—
      "Welcome to the human race.
         The only people I know
            who *don't* have problems
               are in places like
                  Sunset Memorial Park."
To live
   invites problems.
      To dream
         invites problems.
            To venture
               invites problems.
                  To risk
                     invites problems.
But problems are not intruders
   or destroyers of life;
      neither are they surprises
         or exceptions.
Problems are a *part* of life.
   We ought to expect them
      just as surely as we expect happiness.
Problems can be doorways
   to new opportunities,
      springboards
         to launch us into new
            surprising horizons.
If you have problems
   you have new opportunities.
The only thing more deadly to you

than problems could ever be
   is uninterrupted
      uninspiring
         comfort.
When you think you have no problems,
   you really have them!

Think of an eagle,
   her nest high in the mountain crags
      overlooking a peaceful valley.
   She lays her eggs in the nest
      and protects them with her life—
         keeping them warm through the cold nights,
         sheltering them from bad weather.
One day the shells begin to crack
   and new life appears.
      The young eaglets discover the comfort and warmth
        and security and joy
           of their world—
              the mass of honeycombed twigs and feathers.
When their little bellies cry for food
   they squawk
      and before long
         their mother hovers over them
           with breakfast—
              a rabbit clutched in her talons.
She tears the furry creature in pieces
   and feeds her family.
When the storm clouds gather,
   she gathers her young beneath her wings.
      When it is chilly,
         they cuddle close to her
           and feel the warm heartbeat
           of her love.
Days turn to weeks
   and weeks to months
      while the eaglets grow—
         knowing nothing but the comfort
         of their home,

MAKE IT HAPPEN!

the security of parents
who take care of all their needs.
They seem to have no problems at all.
If they continue without problems,
they will face one of the greatest tragedies
living creatures could possibly face—
never to discover the destiny
for which they have been created.
Soon they are feathered out—
still content to have their mother feed and care for them.
But then one day
she seems to go crazy.
She tears the nest apart—
there goes their home,
their security.
She flutters over them
beating her wings
as if hoping her young will imitate her
but they don't.
She perches on the rocky ledge
and lets one of her young climb on her back
as they have done in playful moments in the past.
But this time
she catapults herself off the side of the cliff.
With her massive wings
she climbs higher and higher,
her fear-petrified offspring
clinging to her back for all it's worth.
When she reaches a fantastic altitude,
she shifts
pitches
and throws him free.
The startled eaglet plummets through space
begins to beat his wings
furiously in fright
and suddenly discovers
that the currents beneath
can lift him.
That day
he discovers new horizons,

new reasons for being,
   in the miracle of flight.
The miracle would never have happened
  if his security had not been disturbed,
    if he had not been confronted
      with a problem.
The mother eagle returns
  and takes the second eaglet on her back
    in the same way.
She soars high into the sky
  throws him off
    and he plummets toward the earth below,
      beating his wings furiously—
But he hasn't mastered the miracle of flight
  and he's heading for his death
    on the rocks below
      until his mother dives at a reckless speed
        passes her plummeting offspring
        spreads her wings
          catches him on her pinions
          and lifts him up again.
She goes through the same procedure
  over and over
    until he, too, finally masters
      the miracle of flight.

God allows things to stir up our nests, too,
  lets us get a bit uncomfortable,
    allows problems so that we
      might learn the miracle of flight.
Problems are not enemies.
  They can be gateways
    to greater things.
      Problems and difficulties
        are at the very heart of real living.
Learn how to deal with them.
  Realize that every problem
    is an opportunity
      to learn something.
The fear and confusion of the little eagles

when their mother started tearing their home apart
must have been terrific.
Imagine their reaction:
"Hey, mother!
What are you doing?
You're going nuts!
You're tearing our world apart!"
In that moment
they must have felt
that nothing made sense.
Is it so different with us?
Problems roll in
and we go under.
Nine out of ten of us
would like to throw in the towel
and quit.
But the list is endless
of men and women
who have seen dreams shattered
confronted a blank wall
been overwhelmed with problems
and felt they had reached the end of the road
only to discover
that the problem was a stepping-stone
to new ventures,
new discoveries,
a larger life.
Whether your problems are physical limitations
or marital problems,
whether death has robbed you
or finances have encumbered you—
whatever the problem is
you can turn it into an opportunity
if you want to.
As with the eagle,
when life stirs your nest
the stirring can be a springboard
to a new and larger life.
It isn't by chance

that this great nation
  has chosen the eagle as its symbol.
When the storm strikes
  the eagle doesn't fight it,
    doesn't run from it.
      He sets his wings
        and slowly but surely
          the current raises him higher and higher
            until he literally soars over it.
When your nest is stirred up
  and you are thrust into the mystery of flight,
    never fear.
      Even if you falter,
        the everlasting arms will hold you
          until you, too,
            seize the opportunity
              to discover the miracle of flight.

Opportunities in
Failure

On a hunting trip
  high in the mountains
    we came to an abandoned mining town.
      I sat on my horse
        and looked around.
The mountains were honeycombed with mines,
  the homes dilapidated and empty,
    the streets echoing and bare.
"How dumb can you get?"
  I asked myself.
    "How could anyone leave everything they had
      to come to a place like this
        and call it living?"
I saw nothing
  but shattered dreams
    empty hopes
      frustrated ambition
        failure.
For all their energy and effort
  and eighteen-hours-a-day labor,
    ninety-nine and forty-four one-hundredths percent
      of the gold seekers
        ended up with only an empty hole in the ground.
I sat there
  shaking my head at the broken dreams,
    having risked nothing more
      than a Sunday morning horseback ride
        in the mountains.
We're like that—
  looking at people
    from our smug

comfortable
  security-oriented positions
    saying—
      "It doesn't make sense.
        How could you subject your families
          to all that inconvenience
            all that suffering—
              even to death—
                for nothing?"
We are so isolated
  so insulated by our self-righteousness
    that we can't hear
      the roar of their laughter
        as it comes out of every mine
          every vacant house
            every empty street.
They laugh and say—
  "You're the fools.
    You're the dummies.
      You're the poor excuses for human beings.
      At least we tried."

The fear of failure
  is fast infecting this entire nation of ours.
    Nobody wants to fail.
      We are a success-oriented people.
        Success is what makes sense of everything.
        Success motivates us.
But there is something far more deadly than failing—
  not trying.
Look at Moses.
  He was challenged by God
    to do something he didn't want to do.
      He was asked to go into the land of Egypt
        and lead the people to the Promised Land.
Moses went to God with all kinds of excuses—
  "God, they won't listen to me.
    Who am I, anyway?
      What's going to convince them
        that I have the authority

           to speak to royalty?
                Besides, I've got a speech impediment."
God grew angry with Moses and said—
    "Look, I'll let your brother Aaron
        go with you.
            He can be the mouthpiece."
But Moses still made all sorts of excuses.
    He didn't want to go.
        He was married and had a house
            a family and security
                and he liked what he had.
                    He didn't want to risk all that
                        to do what God wanted him to do.
Moses was afraid to fail
    and so he presented all sorts of reasons
        why he shouldn't even try.
We're like that.
    We're afraid of failure
        so we dream up all kinds of excuses
            for not trying.
            They are carefully designed
                to protect us from the embarrassment
                of failure.
The ability to handle failure
    is not part of our equipment.
        We have not learned how to fail,
            how to accept failure
                as an integral part of success.
Here are three simple tools
    that will help you handle failure:
First:
    Expect to fail
        in some of the things you do.
            The only guy who wins them all
              is the guy who plays by himself
              and cheats.
            In life you can't win them all.
              Life's going to let you win some
                and lose some.

Second:
Never see failure
as an indication of your lack of value.
Invariably, when we fail
we are convinced that we are no good.
This is pure stupidity.
Anyone who risks,
anyone who reaches,
anyone who tries something
might fail.
I had a friend in the Second World War.
He saw some of his friends in trouble
and he tried to help them.
As he tried
he got hit.
He didn't achieve his objective
but they gave him a medal for failing.
Most of the people who got purple hearts
never walked into Berlin
never walked into Tokyo
never saw their dreams fulfilled,
but they received medals
because they tried.
Failure is never an indication that you lack value.
It is an indication that you *have* value,
that you are willing to try.
Third:
Analyze your failure.
It's hard to do.
When I fail I don't want to think about it.
I worry about what my wife is going to think
what my family will think
what my kids will think.
I want to take my failure
and push it to the farthest recesses
of my memory.
But that's wrong.
I must accept failure
as a part of my life.
I must look at it

and say to myself
"Why did I fail?
What should I have done differently?
Where can I make adjustments?
What can I learn from it
so that next time
I won't fail?"
Don't sit and lick your wounds
letting life walk by you.
Analyze your failures.
Make them tools
for the next adventure of life.
Some of God's greatest people
have been lifted out of the ashes of failure.
Listen to this one:
Failed in business '31
Failed for legislature '32
Failed in business '33
Suffered nervous breakdown '36
Failed as Speaker '38
Failed as Elector '40
Failed for Congress '43
Failed for Senate '55
Failed for Vice-Presidency '56
Failed for Senate '58.
Elected President of these United States '60.
His name was Abraham Lincoln.
An opportunity attitude
looks beyond failure
sees the things that could be
reaches out for them
and grasps them.
An opportunity attitude
is not something you're born with;
it's something you teach yourself.
If you can tell yourself that life is lousy,
that you've been treated miserably,
you can turn your attitude around
and train yourself to see
the opportunities God gives you.

God asks us to believe him
　trust him
　　follow him.
　　　He asks us to realize
　　　　that when he works with us and in us,
　　　　　there are no limits to what we can do.
Even if we fail,
　even if we fall short,
　　God is not licked.
　　　The fulfillment of the promise
　　　can yet be ours.
Don't you feel the excitement?
　Don't you want to change the way you think
　　and live
　　　and move?
You who name the name of Christ,
　you who believe the eternal God cares about you,
　　look up
　　　and begin to realize that
　　　　the opportunities he offers you
　　　　are infinite.
Don't look at failure;
　look at him!
　　Take hold of the opportunity he hands you
　　　—and try!